Shani King

Have I Ever Told You?

Illustrations by Anna Horváth

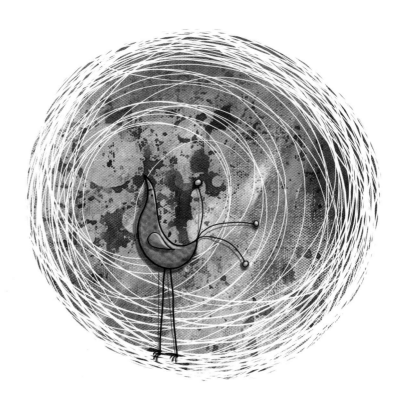

To my kids, Soraya and Matias.

—S. K.

To my children, Máté and Kinga

—A. H.

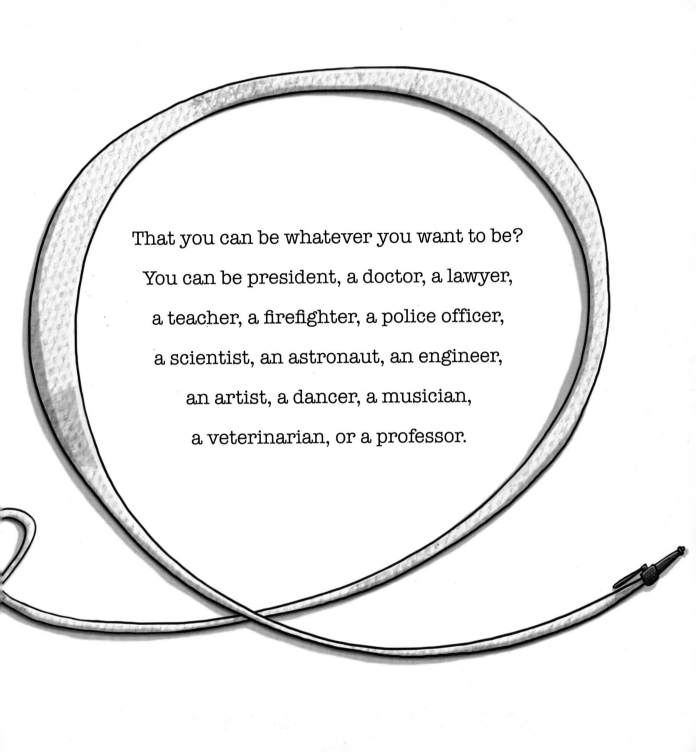

That you can be whatever you want to be?

You can be president, a doctor, a lawyer,

a teacher, a firefighter, a police officer,

a scientist, an astronaut, an engineer,

an artist, a dancer, a musician,

a veterinarian, or a professor.

Have I ever told you...

that there are many people

who look just like you,

your skin color, your hair color,

who talk like you do,

who speak Spanish, Arabic, Mandarin, and English,

who are presidents, Supreme Court justices,

who are doctors and lawyers

and teachers and scientists and engineers?

Have I ever told you that?

Have I ever told you that

for me,

there is no one more special than you?

That for me, you are

the most special child in the world,

and that I love you now and will love you forever?

Have I ever told you that?

Have I ever told you that

you make me the happiest person in the world, just by being you?

Have I ever told you that?

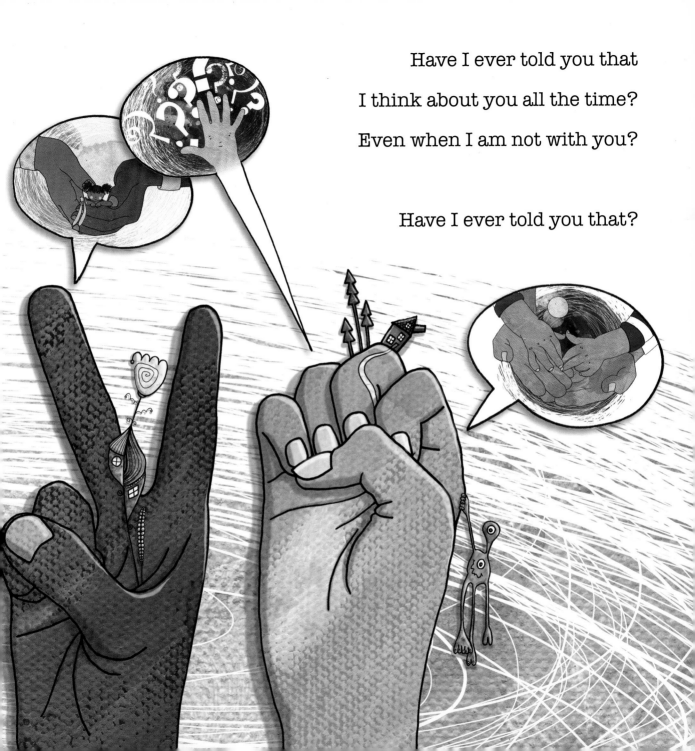

Have I ever told you that
you make me laugh out loud
all the time?

Have I ever told you that I love
the stories you tell
and the conversations
we have?
That I love
to listen to you
and talk to you?

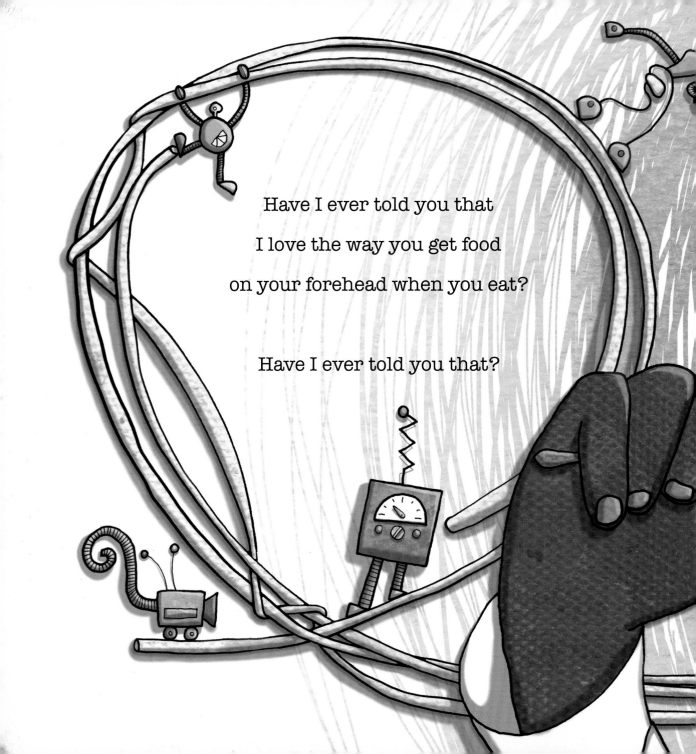

Have I ever told you that

I love the way you get food

on your forehead when you eat?

Have I ever told you that?

Have I ever told you that
I will never let anyone
hurt you or threaten you
without having to
deal with me first?

Have I ever told you that?

Have I ever told you that

if you hear a word

that makes you uncomfortable,

you can ask me what it means

and we can talk about it?

Have I ever told you that?

Have I ever told you that
you should be kind to everyone
and treat everyone with respect—
people who are poor or rich, clean or dirty,
homeless or undocumented, gay or straight?
That we are all equally deserving of respect
because we are all people?
People with friends and families
who love them just like I love you?
Just like your friends love you?

Have I ever told you that?

Have I ever told you that you should stand up

for people who need help,

or are being picked on by others?

People of any color. People of any faith.

People of any size, shape, or ability.

Have I ever told you that?

Have I ever told you that

you should always do the right thing,

even if it's hard?

Have I ever told you that?

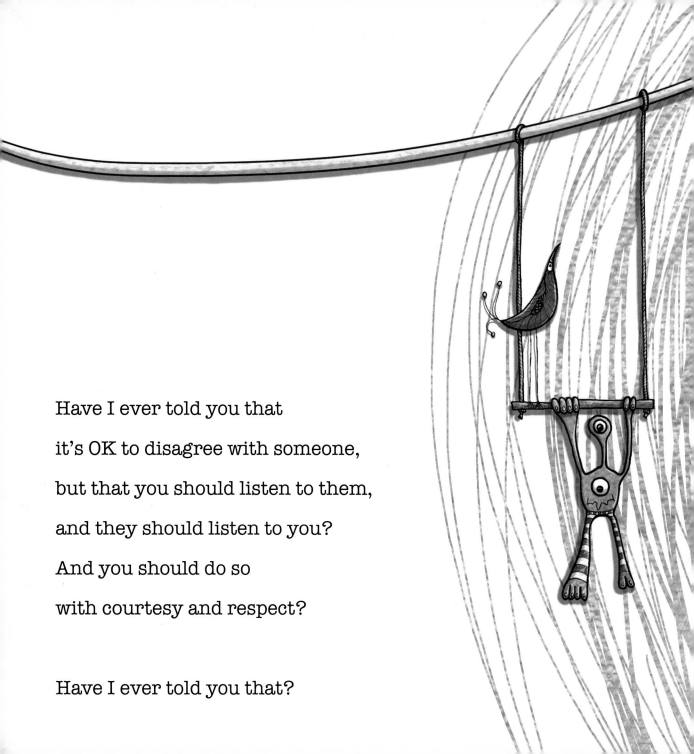

Have I ever told you that

it's OK to disagree with someone,

but that you should listen to them,

and they should listen to you?

And you should do so

with courtesy and respect?

Have I ever told you that?

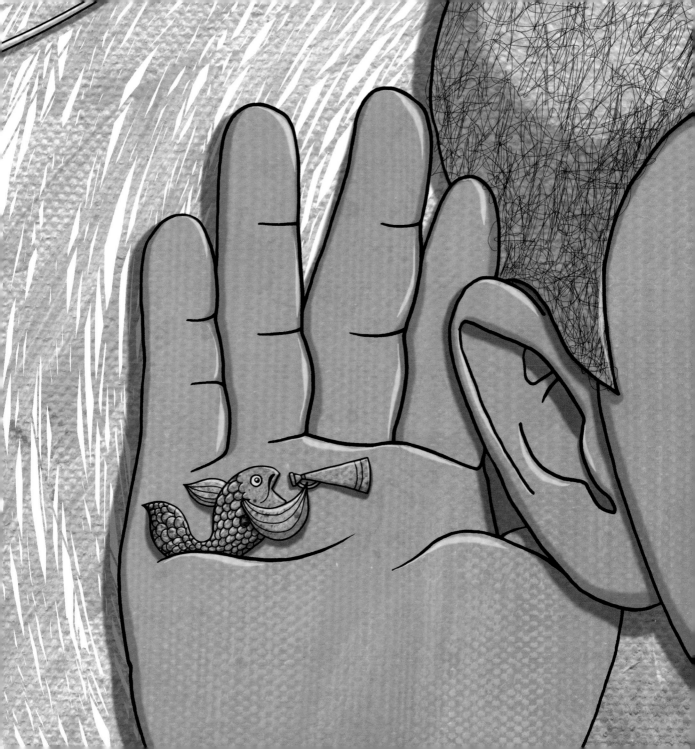

Have I ever told you

that you are courageous, hard-working,

smart, beautiful, handsome, funny, tough,

humble, determined,

patient, honest, compassionate, kind,

curious, positive, thankful,

respectful, and hopeful?

Have I ever told you that?

Have I ever told you that?

Yes, I think I have. And all of that is true.

I love you!

Written by Shani King

Illustrated by Anna Horváth

This project has benefited from the generous support of the Center on Children and Families at the University of Florida Frederic G. Levin College of Law.

ISBN: 978-1-59298-694-1

Library of Congress Catalog Number: 2017913181

Printed in Canada

First Printing: 2018

22 21 20 19 18   5 4 3 2 1

Beaver's Pond Press, Inc.
7108 Ohms Lane
Edina, MN 55439–2129

(952) 829-8818

www.BeaversPondPress.com

To order, visit www.ItascaBooks.com or call
1-800-901-3480 ext. 118. Reseller discounts available.